Satin Dolls
THE WOMEN OF JAZZ

The Life, Times, & Music™ Series

Satin Dolls
THE WOMEN OF JAZZ

The Life, Times, & Music™ Series

Andrew G. Hager

FRIEDMAN/FAIRFAX

PUBLISHERS

A FRIEDMAN GROUP BOOK

ISBN 1-56799-132-7

THE LIFE, TIMES, & MUSIC™ SERIES
SATIN DOLLS: The Women of Jazz
was prepared and produced by
Michael Friedman Publishing Group, Inc.
15 West 26th Street
New York, New York 10010

Editor: Nathaniel Marunas
Art Director: Jeff Batzli
Designer: Patrick McCarthy
Photography Editor: Colleen Branigan

Grateful acknowledgment is given to authors, publishers, and photographers for permission to reprint material. Every effort has been made to determine copyright owners of photographs and illustrations. In the case of any omissions, the publishers will be pleased to make suitable acknowledgments in future editions.

Printed in the United States of America

For bulk purchases and special sales, please contact:
Friedman/Fairfax Publishers
Attention: Sales Department
15 West 26th Street
New York, New York 10010
(212) 685-6610 FAX (212) 685-1307

Acknowledgments

Special thanks to composer and jazz historian Fred Carl and to poet and playwright Hattie Gossett.

Dedication

Thanks for the hazelnut coffee, Sherry and Marty.

Sarah Vaughan.

CONTENTS

Introduction

Instrumental jazz and female singers were brought together by the combined influence of several different musical idioms. Blues, Dixieland, ragtime, West Indian rhythms, European song form, and early African-American musical theatre each played a part in the evolution of the female jazz vocalist.

The primary roles that women have played in popular jazz have been as singers. Their function, when they were first allowed to the stage, was to balance through popular song form the technically advanced compositional and improvisational skills of the male instrumentalists. As the relationship between vocalists and instrumentalists grew, the female singers' duties expanded.

Over a period of six decades, the women of jazz fought for and eventually gained the right to participate fully in the music business, based on personal ability and collaborative know-how.

In Webster's dictionary, one of the definitions of *jazz*, which typically misses the point, is "a sexual term applied to the Congo dance." Besides being an alarmist oversimplification, this definition is very dated, failing as it does even to touch on the many transformations the music has undergone over the years. However negative its formal connotations, though, the word *jazz* has been used colloquially over time by devotees in a flexible manner that more accurately reflects the changeable nature of the music itself. It should come as no surprise that the word for the music that gave the United States its international artistic identity has been both defined and defiled by the skewed politics of gender and race.

The Blues

The secular kin to black gospel music, the blues has played a key role in the ever-changing form of twentieth-century music as well as in the development of the female singer as a viable commercial recording artist.

The role of the female blues singer, from the turn of the century until the advent of popular jazz in the late 1910s and 1920s, went through its own dramatic evolution, drawing on other forms of popular entertainment like vaudeville, minstrelsy, and the Broadway extravaganza.

By 1920, female blues vocalists began making headway into commercial music. Mamie Smith (1883–1946), one of five unrelated successful blues singers of the era with the same last name, is credited with the first blues hit, "Crazy Blues," recorded on the OK/Phonola label. The record sold thousands of copies, inaugurating the era of the "race record."

The increasing popularity of the black female singer/entertainer would soon bring many such women to the Broadway stage.

Ragtime

Contrary to several musicians' claims of having invented jazz, the music evolved because of the efforts of an entire community. For instance, the technical advances made by instrumental musicians in ragtime music that played a major role in the development of jazz (both improvisationally and rhythmically) occurred in three separate parts of the country at about the same time. Two people are specifically credited with making the transition from ragtime to jazz.

The most notorious of the two innovators was pianist and pool hustler Jelly Roll Morton (1890–1941). Born Ferdinand Joseph LaMenthe, Morton was the Creole son of one of the wealthiest businessmen in New Orleans. Being part of the upper-class Creole culture (Creoles are a blend of French, African-American, and Native American blood) in New

Though he first learned to play the guitar, Jelly Roll Morton launched his tumultuous career playing the piano in bars in his native New Orleans.

Orleans, Morton's parents saw to it that their son's early musical training was primarily classical European. He studied the violin, guitar, trombone, and, from the age of eleven on, the piano. All of the lessons were taught to him in his first language, French.

Soon after his mother's death, when Morton was only fourteen, he began playing the piano in various seedy establishments in New Orleans' Tenderloin district. His grandmother, a well-respected socialite, did not approve of music as a profession; nor did she appreciate her grandchild's fraternization with hoodlums in the venues where popular music was played. By the end of that year Morton was forced from his home, and he began hustling for money while moving from state to state.

By 1923, Jelly Roll Morton had recorded his first piano solos, and within the next three years recorded the famous Red Hot Peppers sessions that led to his extensive national touring.

Morton's style of dress (flashy clothes and a diamond-inlaid tooth) and his musical dexterity blurred the line separating popular entertainment and art, making him one of the most provocative and successful entertainers in Chicago during the 1920s.

By 1930, the audience that had hailed him as the king of ragtime and one of the forefathers of jazz had moved on to newer, more popular dance music, leaving him penniless and nearly forgotten. The last years of his life were spent in costly lawsuits and failed attempts at a comeback. Until the day he died, Jelly Roll Morton would tell anyone who would listen how he, alone, had invented jazz.

The humble and nearly forgotten father of the Harlem, or East Coast, stride school is James P. Johnson (1894–1955). Very little is known about the personal life of the soft-spoken Johnson. The date of his birth is disputed, James himself believing he was born on February 1, 1894. His brother stated, years after Johnson's death, that he was "sure" James had been born in either 1891 or 1892.

Stride, a style of piano playing based on complex, rhythmic bass patterns played with the left hand, became one of the most important ele-

There has recently been speculation by several jazz historians that the songs "I Got Plenty O' Nuttin'" and "Summertime" were actually penned by James P. Johnson, and later bought by the Gershwins for fifty dollars apiece.

ments of ragtime and early jazz. Like the legendary Scott Joplin (1868–1917) and Morton, James Johnson was a student of both European and African-American musical forms; the mixture of church music, Southern blues, Shout and Stomp, and European classical styles made his brand of music a cornerstone of the growing North American sound. His greatest hit, the "Charleston," is the best-remembered song of the Roaring Twenties. In addition, the most successful African-American musical in the post–*Shuffle Along* heyday, entitled *Runnin' Wild*, was penned by Johnson. He also wrote several symphonies, concertos, tone poems, and even an opera.

From the 1940s forward Johnson composed only sporadically and made few recordings. A series of strokes ultimately left him paralyzed and bedridden until his death in November 1955, at his home in Jamaica, Queens, New York.

Díxíeland

New Orleans' rich musical tradition also played an important role in the development of jazz. Even before the appearance of Jelly Roll Morton in Chicago, Creole ensembles had made their way both westward and northward, popularizing the music of the Crescent City.

The first of many of these Creole Dixieland musicians was bassist, guitarist, and banjo player Bill Johnson. His band, the Original Creole Orchestra, included several brass instrumentalists. George Baquet, who played the clarinet (a central instrument of the early Dixieland sound), and Ernest Coycault, the cornetist, were key players in the Creole Orchestra. The group toured the South extensively until 1907, when they reached the West Coast music scene and were greeted with success. By 1914, the band had gone on the vaudeville circuit across North America, and in the following year made its New York debut at the Winter Garden. By 1917, the "new" sound of the Original Creole Orchestra had become so popular that there were then six Creole bands touring across the United States. By World War I, the Dixieland craze had inspired many California musicians to become professional players of the New Orleans sound.

During this period, African-Americans migrated in enormous numbers from the rural South to the thriving urban centers of the North, where unheard-of salaries in the factories and foundries awaited them. Black musicians followed this route, too, because they could make much more money in the Northern cities than they could at home in the South. Many bands from Louisiana, such as the Original Dixieland Jazz Band and the ensembles of Jack Bechet and King Oliver (1885–1939), began making headway in the burgeoning Chicago music industry.

African-American Musical Theatre

Before the Gershwins, Rodgers, Hart, Hammerstein, and the Golden Age of Broadway in general, the history of successful musical theatre from the 1890s to the 1920s included many successful musicals and revues written and performed by African-Americans. These black composers and performers paid homage to the style of theatre then in vogue with white Americans while breaking new ground by introducing their own, syncopated music into the mix. The black female singers who partici-pated in this early form of North American musical theatre would soon cross over into jazz, permanently linking the history of popular song form with the history of instrumental jazz.

Bessie Smith was a talented and deter-mined woman whose success paved the way for female vocalists to come.

In 1890, the Census Bureau counted 1,490 black actors touring with minstrel companies across the United States. The incredible Bessie Smith, W. C. Handy (1873–1958), and Bert Williams (1874–1922) were just a few of the black entertainers who honed their skills on the min-strel and vaudeville circuits. The minstrel-show format became so popular by the 1890s that white pro-ducers began to jump on the band-wagon, casting white performers in black makeup to mimic the African-American minstrel acts. Although white interest in black entertainment was made obvious by this mimicry, only one show written and performed by an African-American was able to gain success in New York (Off Broadway) during this time: *All Coons Look Alike To Me,* by Ernest Hogan.

The first black actress to taste success on the New York stage was Sissieritta Jones. Her career began in 1892 with the *Jubilee Spectacle and*

Bessie Smith (1894–1937)

The "Empress of the Blues," Bessie Smith was once described by her fan and friend George Avakian as "an artist of impeccable taste, with a huge sweeping voice which combined strength and even harshness with irresistible beauty." The recordings that are left of her powerful talents are a testament to this statement, and remain as intimate and overwhelming as the day they were recorded.

In her early teens, singer and songwriter Bessie Smith left the brutal poverty of her Chattanooga, Tennessee, home forever to go on the road with Ma Rainey's Rabbit Foot Minstrels. Years of work in honky tonks, carnivals, and tent shows followed. Smith was finally "discovered" by Frank Walker, the recording director for Columbia Records, in a Selma, Alabama, club.

With the help of Walker and composer-pianist Clarence Williams, Smith was able to make her first recordings on February 17, 1923, in New York City. One year later Smith had already sold an overwhelming two million records, and had become a headliner on the vaudeville circuit.

From the years 1924 to 1927 Smith became one of the most successful black entertainers in the United States, frequently appearing with the likes of Louis Armstrong, Don Redman, James P. Johnson, and Fletcher Henderson. Her marriage to Jack Gee, a policeman who became the full-time manager of his new wife's career, came at the height of her popularity.

By 1930, alcoholism, combined with a lack of good material and the ever-changing taste of music consumers, removed her from the public eye. She continued to tour the vaudeville circuit with her own company, the Midnight Steppers, with some success. The highlight of her post-heyday was an appearance in the Warner Brothers movie St. Louis Blues in 1933.

Just days before a recording date in New York City, in September 1937, Smith was in a serious car accident and needed immediate medical attention. The hospital she was first sent to refused her admission because of her race, and on the way to another hospital she bled to death.

Cakewalk, which was performed at Madison Square Garden. An opera singer by training, Jones (dubbed "Black Patti" by the critics because her talents rivaled those of the famed Italian singer Adelina Patti) performed during her career at the White House reception for President Harrison, and later toured extensively throughout Europe. The shows she was able to work in after her successful European tour were still based on producers' misperceptions about what (paying) white audiences wanted to see. (A highlight of her post–European tour career, for instance, was the starring role in a mini-musical written by Bob Cole entitled *At Jolly Coon-ey Island.*)

The first round of successful touring musicals written and performed by African-Americans was a series of shows that shared the same setting, Coontown (in some of these shows called Jimtown). *A Trip to Coontown, Clorindy*, and *Jes Lak White Folks* helped introduce the syncopated music of the black tradition to the stage. Performed by black actors, dancers, and singers, these traveling shows helped promote this unique amalgam of blues and musical comedy, which in turn influenced the development of the jazz idiom. Furthermore, performers such as Jones established a precedent for commercially successful female entertainers.

Between 1910 and 1917 black musical theatre history seemed to be drawing to a close. Had it not been for the success of *Shuffle Along* in late 1921—with its astounding 540-performance run—the history of jazz might have unfolded very differently.

By late 1922, only one year after *Shuffle Along*, the success of African-Americans on Broadway began to raise eyebrows. With the help of successful blues performers, the commercial recording industry and the Broadway stage joined forces, creating the early black female stars. Ethel Waters appeared in two very successful shows, *Oh Joy* and *Cabin in the Sky*; Edith Wilson and Florence Mills were showcased in *Plantation Revue*; Eva Taylor starred in *Bottomland*; and the late, great Alberta Hunter (1895–1984) was featured in the musical *Change Your Luck*.

Ethel Waters (1900–1977)

At the age of five Ethel Waters made her singing debut in her hometown of Chester, Pennsylvania, billed as "Baby Star." By her early teens the tall and extremely thin Waters was billed as "Sweet Mama Stringbean," and performed in Philadelphia and Baltimore clubs. At the age of seventeen, when the nation was embroiled in World War I, she moved to New York City and began working at the Lincoln Theatre in Harlem, a club now legendary for promoting the careers of many of jazz's early artists. By the 1920s Waters had gained success as a popular "race recording" artist for Black Swan and Columbia. Her earliest live entertainment work began in 1924 as a replacement for Florence Mills in a show that had become popularized by its then-risqué integrated cast, *Plantation Revue*.

After Mills returned to the show, Waters went on the road as a lead in *Calico*, a popular cabaret. Its producer, Earl Dancer, was so taken by her performance that he convinced banker Otto H. Kahn to put up ten thousand dollars for a musical that would star the talented young Waters called *Africana*.

The second act almost entirely focused on her hit songs "Dinah," "Shake That Thing," "Take Your Black Bottom Outside," and "I'm Coming Virginia."

Although the show was a financial failure (it was performed in an empty lot when it reached New York), Waters had gained enough notoriety to bring her into the cast of the most popular show starring an all-black cast of the 1920s, *Cabin in the Sky*. In 1933 her relationship to musical theatre was again furthered by her appearance in Irving Berlin's successful production *As Thousands Cheer*.

Ethel Waters parlayed her experience in vaudeville and musical comedy into a career as a successful recording artist. She was instrumental in bringing the achievements of early jazz artists, then only distributed on race labels, to the eyes and ears of white audiences. Thanks to her great sense for business, a bigger-than-life personality, and diverse talents, white audiences began demanding the unique artistic output of black artists early on in the twentieth century.

After forty-four years of success as a singer on Broadway, in film, and on the radio, Alberta Hunter attended school for nursing, then went to work at Memorial Hospital on Welfare Island, New York City.

This first substantial African-American success in the entertainment business led to an unsubstantiated fear among most of Broadway's white producers that the rise of popular black theatrical culture would cause diminishing financial returns for shows written and performed by whites. The directors of the Ziegfeld Follies, now remembered as the "rage" of Broadway during this decade, began a campaign against the public's growing taste for African-American musical theatre on June 5, 1922. Gilda Fray (one of Ziegfeld's finest leading ladies) started off the evening's show with the following lines, which underline both the racism and commercialism of the times:

> *It's getting very dark on ol' Broadway*
> *Just like an eclipse of the moon*

Ev'ry cafe now has the dancing coon.

Pretty chocolate babies

Shake and shimmie ev'rywhere

Real dark-town entertainers hold the stage

You must black-up to be the latest rage

Yes, the great white way is white no more,

It's just like a street on the Swanee shore.

The many African-American instrumental bands playing across the country were also aware of the success of black singers and songwriters in musical theatre, and these instrumentalists began to make efforts to link the success of one idiom to the other.

Ethel Waters and Buck Bubbles dance to the music of Duke Ellington in the classic MGM film Cabin in the Sky.

Shuffle Along

The year 1921 was financially rough for New York City. Retail stores laid off hundreds of employees, and by doing so frightened the city's entertainment industry out of promoting too many new productions (these employees constituted the theatre-going crowds). Broadway producers in particular played it safe and decided to mount only new shows through the month of May, a full month short of the regular production schedule. For a show to come off the road and into the Big Apple in this risky financial climate was considered foolish; for a musical written and performed by African-Americans to brave this storm was double jeopardy.

Shuffle Along, with lyrics by Noble Sissle (1889–1975) and music by Eubie Blake (1883–1992), faced not only these challenges but also a dreaded June premiere. Already eighteen thousand dollars in debt from a brief northeastern tour, the company of black performers and writers ignored all warnings, sure that the show would be well received.

The instantaneous and overwhelming success of Shuffle Along, which enjoyed a total of 540 performances, spawned more than just the hit song "I'm Just Wild About Harry." For the first time, African-American entertainers had dispelled the producer-promoted misperception that white audiences would not go to see shows written and performed by blacks. By disproving the myth, Shuffle Along spawned a decade of successful African-American musicals, created the first black stars, and as Langston Hughes (1902–1967) once pointed out, ignited the Harlem Renaissance. (Hughes also stated that he originally decided to attend Columbia University because he would then be able to see Sissle and Blake's show.)

Flournoy Miller and Aubrey Lyles, the writers of the script and the leads of the

Eubie Blake and Noble Sissle are credited with breaking through the color barrier and onto the Great White Way.

show, were catapulted into the limelight. The duo, both graduates of Fisk University, would have continued success throughout the 1920s. Even the replacement cast members for *Shuffle Along* were to become stars in their own right. The sensuous Josephine Baker (1906–1975), a chorus girl in the secondary cast, was one of the most recognizable figures of the 1920s entertainment industry. In addition, the lawyer, athlete, singer, actor, and activist Paul Robeson (1898–1976) and the first black female superstar, Adelaide Hall, found their early success as members of the cast.

Two of the earliest African-American superstars, Paul Robeson (left) and Josephine Baker (above) began their acting careers in the chorus of Shuffle Along.

The shows that followed in the footsteps of Sissle and Blake's success expanded on the rhythmic vocabulary of ragtime made popular by *Shuffle Along*, and also set the stage for the ascendance of the first round of jazz singers like Alberta Hunter and Ethel Waters, whose performances were a blend of Broadway bravura and blues-based singing.

After fifteen years of overwhelming success as an actress and singer on the black vaudeville circuit, Adelaide Hall moved to England to escape racism.

Testing the Waters

As early as 1918, vocalists made their first appearance in instrumental ensembles; bandleaders incorporated the singer as part of the brass, reed, or rhythm section of the band. The singers were hired to handle only the refrains between instrumental solos. Joseph C. Smith's orchestra is the first recorded example of this emerging relationship. A trio made up of

Harry McDonough, Charles Hart, and Lewis James was hired to sing the refrain of Smith's popular song "Mary."

One of the only women to make it to the stage with a band during this early period of vocalist involvement was singer-actress Nora Bayes (1880–1928), who was hired with singer Frank Crumit to record two songs on Columbia Records with Art Hickman and his orchestra.

Changing Technology

Until the invention of the microphone, singing in front of a twenty-piece band involved certain practical problems. The difficulty of being heard over the brass section was, in and of itself, a dilemma that kept the early band singer in a second-class position. The advent of the microphone did not, however, immediately solve this problem. In fact, the new technology added another stumbling block: Vocalists who could belt out songs loudly enough to be heard over these early bands had a hard time adjusting to the new equipment. As was true with the talking movies, the microphone displaced many early performing professionals who proved unable to adapt to the sensitive new instrument. Establishing a working relationship between the microphone and the voice proved to be a craft in itself. Thus, many singers of the period were never able to make the transition effectively. Those vocalists who were able to achieve success during the early post-microphone era, however, proved to the bandleaders that the singer could be a qualified, collaborating musician in the band. The microphone also created opportunities for female singers in general; a female vocalist sounded brash trying to sing over a band until this technology, which allowed for greater subtlety, arose.

A professional performer since the age of five, Ethel Waters was first billed as "Sweet Mama Stringbean" thanks to her waifish appearance.

Cliff Edwards, one of several of the early post-microphone jazz singers, began his career in the 1910s working for silent movie houses as accompanist to the feature films. Singing while playing his ukulele, Edwards created many unusual vocal sound effects (a technique that he termed "eefin'"), which are the earliest examples of scat singing in recording history. Like Bobby McFerrin today, Edwards could impersonate an entire orchestra with his voice. The introduction of the microphone was no hindrance to Edwards' bluesy style, and in fact allowed him to make greater vocal leaps and craft more unusual tones without harming his voice. His first recording, James P. Johnson's "Old Fashioned Love," shows off his vocal dexterity with an opening "trumpet" solo that was, understandably, mistaken by listeners for the real thing. Although Edwards' contribution to early jazz is virtually forgotten, his later work in film overdubbing (specifically as Jiminy Cricket singing "If You Wish Upon a Star") is remembered by almost everyone.

Louis Armstrong (1900–1971), trumpeter, singer, and bandleader, cut the song "Heebie Jeebies" in 1926, legitimizing the pop-jazz singing school almost single-handedly. So popular was Armstrong's singing that within a few months white bandleader Paul Whiteman (1890–1967) introduced a vocal trio to his staff of musicians, led by none other than Bing Crosby (1904–1977).

Although many people who grew up watching Crosby's movies from the 1940s and 1950s think of him as a popular matinee idol, his contributions to jazz are invaluable. From the 1920s until the late 1940s his ease with the microphone and conversation-volume singing, in addition to his overall musical dexterity, made him the most impersonated singer of the early twentieth century. As singing legend Jimmy Rushing (1903–1972) once stated, most singers of the dance-band era were either "a high Bing or a low Bing." Crosby's greatest contribution to the era was the final amalgamation of jazz music with the popular songs of Tin Pan Alley.

The most important of the female jazz singers of the 1920s was Annette Hanshaw (1910–1985). Her confident interpretation of songs

was grounded by an inherent feel for the rhythmic underpinnings of swing and blues. Her interest in the music was all-encompassing, and by the time she was eighteen, her father, a wealthy hotel owner, had bought her a music shop. He also hired her to sing regularly at hotel engagements.

Pathe Records talent scout Wally Rose "discovered" Hanshaw at one of these hotel gigs and quickly signed her to the label. The young Hanshaw, along with Cliff Edwards, became the leading attraction of the Pathe label.

Sadly, the jazz idiom bene-fitted from the talents of Annette Hanshaw, one of the genre's earliest female stars, for only a short period of time. Hanshaw was not pre-pared for fame and all its trap-pings. Tired of the publicity, the hectic touring schedules, and the inability to lead a nor-mal life, Hanshaw retired from her career in music forever at the age of twenty-eight.

If it hadn't been for Hanshaw, the early history of jazz singing would have been almost entire-ly made up of men. Her con-siderable ability and conse-

Above, top: Louis Armstrong and Martha Raye perform in a celluloid duet. Above: Uncomfortable with the trappings of public life, the talented Annette Hanshaw retired from singing at the modest age of twenty-eight.

quent influence on the record-buying population changed the public's perception of who could and should sing jazz. As it turned out, the lead singers for nearly all the big bands during the thirties were women.

Breakthrough

Jack Kapp (1901–1949), the most influential and notoriously unmusical talent manager and producer of early jazz, took a chance and placed singer Mildred Bailey, dressed to the nines, in front of the Casa Loma Orchestra to perform four popular numbers that consisted of eight-bar instrumental solos between sung verses. Kapp had long held the belief that if female singers became stars in their own right, then the value of the bands that featured these women as a whole would naturally multiply. Proof of Kapp's hypothesis soon followed when Bailey had her first hit, "Rockin' Chair," recorded with a faction of the most popular of the early bands, Paul Whiteman's orchestra.

Because of the overwhelming success of Bailey in 1931, many female singers working in the industry finally gained popularity. The Boswell sisters' trio and Lee Wiley (1910–1975) jumped into the musical limelight and became the most popular female singers of the early 1930s.

The Boswell Sisters—Martha, Vet, and Connee—were influenced by both the rich musical heritage of their hometown, New Orleans, and many of their close relatives, who were professional musicians themselves. The Boswells' mother, father, aunt, and uncle (the women were sisters and

With the aid of producer Jack Kapp, Mildred Bailey became the first female solo jazz singing star.

Mildred Bailey (1907–1951)

Born Mildred Rinker in Spokane, Washington, the first lady of jazz was one of four siblings who found careers in music. Her brothers, Al, Charles, and Miles—all of whom began as musicians—ultimately worked on the business end of the music industry, as a radio producer, song publisher, and booking agent, respectively.

After the death of their mother, when Mildred was only fourteen, the family moved to Seattle. Soon after that, they moved to Los Angeles, where Mildred found her first job as a song demonstrator. Her brothers befriended the young Bing Crosby, who in turn ultimately helped the two younger brothers find success in radio as a singing team. Mildred also began working with radio station KMTR while in Los Angeles, and soon

after began her famous work with Paul Whiteman's orchestra. "Rockin' Chair," recorded in 1932, made Mildred Bailey the first universally popular female jazz singer. That same year, Bailey wed her third husband—she was twenty-five years old.

Bailey's greatest recording work was undertaken in collaboration with her third husband, bandleader and vibraphonist Red Norvo (1908–). With the help of Jack Kapp's marketing abilities, the duo became known as "Mr. and Mrs. Swing." Arranger Eddie Sauter (1914–1981) joined the team and assisted in putting together some of the finest orchestral arrangements for vocal jazz.

Both the band and the marriage failed between 1939 and 1940. One of several serious illnesses, brought on by years of constant traveling, began to plague Bailey. Her first post-Norvo work was with Benny Goodman's band. Soon after that, she began an unfruitful solo recording career.

CBS Records took a chance on her in 1944, when the label signed Bailey to sing with Paul Barron's swing band on the most popular radio show of the World War II era. By 1949, however, illness had nearly consumed Bailey, forcing her into semiretirement. She was able to make it to Los Angeles for a small amount of recording work and an appearance on Bing Crosby's television show. Mildred Bailey died soon after that excursion, in a hospital near her home in Poughkeepsie, New York, on December 12, 1951.

the men were brothers) sang in a quartet that the Boswell children emulated from an early age. The sisters learned to play a number of instruments: cello, saxophone, violin, and banjo. In homage to her father's music, Vet began playing stride piano.

Having lost three other siblings to illness and war, the remaining members of the Boswell family became very close. The recordings of the Boswell Sisters, with their near-perfect harmonies, still reflect to this day the tight-knit nature of this family.

It is important to note that in the history of trio and quartet singing only three groups were able to achieve technical synchronicity worthy of mentioning as vital to the evolution of jazz. Of the two other important groups, it is no surprise that one, the Mills Brothers, was also family. (Interestingly, the Andrew Sisters could not get along, and this fact is reflected in their music.) The only other trio to make a significant contribution to the jazz idiom—Lambert, Hendrix, and Ross—would not come along for another nineteen years.

While Mildred Bailey brought a charming, ingenuous quality to jazz, and the Boswells demonstrated the merits of near-flawless technical ability, Lee Wiley brought a heartrending honesty to the music; it is a quality that leaves the listener with the impression that Wiley led a very hard life. Her penchant for telling the hard truth, couched in the terms of seduction, makes her one of the earliest examples of the torch singer.

Wiley was born in Fort Gibson, Oklahoma, in either 1910 or 1915 (the exact date is disputed). Her earliest influences were the artists of the "race record" industry: Bessie Smith, Clara Smith (1894–1935), and Ethel Waters. When Wiley was fifteen she ran away from home; in a year's time she was one of the most popular singers in Chicago. At the age of nineteen Wiley moved to New York City (after a year of singing professionally for an Oklahoma radio station). It was in Manhattan where she met bandleader Leo Reisman, who began featuring her on important broadcasts and recordings. She soon received her own radio show, *The Pond's Cold Cream Hour Starring Lee Wiley,* and made several recordings

Lee Wiley's distinctively husky and erotically charged voice made her one of the most popular singers of the day.

backed by the orchestras of the Dorsey Brothers, Casa Loma, Johnny Green, and Paul Whiteman.

Wiley's luck changed for the worse, beginning with a series of illnesses that kept her in and out of the spotlight for the rest of her career. Diagnosed with tuberculosis, Lee lost a year in Arizona "recuperating" from the disease, which she later discovered she'd never actually had. The following year she attempted to find work in California, but while in Los Angeles she contracted a disfiguring eye disease that left her blind for months.

Wiley's career never regained the momentum it had once had, but she was able—thanks to the devotion of several jazz bandleaders—to gain a small, devoted audience over the next two decades. Her work moved

The Boswell Sisters

Relatively early in the history of vocal jazz, three sisters carved out the highest standard in vocal trio music. Their complex, rhythmical, contrapuntal singing—the product of a lifetime collaboration based on mutual admiration—has placed the Boswells above almost every other vocal group in jazz.

The lead singer of the group, Connee (1905–1976), and arranger, Martha (1907–1958), were both born in Kansas City, Missouri. The baby of the group, Vet (1911–1988), was born in Birmingham, Alabama, a few years before the family moved to Louisiana.

Connee was a cripple since childhood. She began taking music lessons at a very early age, first studying the cello and later the piano and other instruments. Sister Vet, an admirer of her father's stride style, became the pianist for the future trio.

Their professional musical career began with concerts given for schools, churches, and local fund-raising campaigns for the all-too-common flood-relief programs. Their philanthropy paid off in local popularity when the sisters were asked to substitute for an act at the famous Orpheum Theatre in 1925. So many members of the Boswells' community came to support the sisters that their act broke all house records for attendance.

Edward King, a local radio disc jockey, heard the girls and got swept up in the growing Boswell craze; he recorded five of their songs. Several vaudeville acts then tried unsuccessfully to sway the Boswells' father into allowing the three girls to go on the road, but to no avail. Not until 1928 did their father grant them permission to leave New Orleans. He gave his blessings (so to speak) to a successful Chicago-based booking agent, who brought the girls first to the Windy City and then to Hollywood for screen tests and their own radio show.

The Boswells' first recordings for a major label were made in March 1930, when Victor Studios Hollywood added the trio to a local dance band for a session. This soon brought them to the attention of producer Jack Kapp, who in the following year landed the Boswells a contract with Brunswick Records in New York. The threesome left Hollywood for New York, and soon after began receiving national airplay on Rudy Vallee's radio show *Fleischmann's Yeast Hour*.

The only element that had been missing from the Boswells' earliest recordings was a high-quality back-up band. In 1939, Brunswick changed all that by hiring extremely talented studio musicians to play behind the Boswells, finally matching the sisters' talent. Eventually, the trio's music would be backed by the incredible orchestras of Benny Goodman, the Dorsey Brothers, Glenn Miller, Bunny Berigan, Joe Venuti, and Eddie Lang.

The trio's disintegration came to pass because the sisters all turned their minds toward the expansion of the family. Vet eloped with a Canadian, John Paul Jones; Connee married their agent, Harry Leedy; and Martha wed George Lloyd, the cofounder of Decca Records' English label.

away from the performance of pop-oriented songs back to jazz-influenced show tunes. In making this shift, Wiley linked the history of female jazz singing to its roots in musical theatre and may have invented the idea of the "standard" (a song that every artist covers). Liberty Records produced several albums with Wiley singing the hits of Cole Porter, the Gershwins, and Rodgers and Hart.

This period in the late 1920s and early 1930s was a turning point in the history of jazz, particularly with regard to the role of the female vocalist. The women of jazz had established at this crucial juncture that the presence of a woman vocalist not only enhanced the popularity of a band, but added another dimension to the music (especially considering Lee Wiley's work in establishing a canon of jazz standards). In the decade to come, these advances were built upon by the next generation of determined and talented female entertainers.

Swing

Until the birth of the rhythmical and musical vocabulary of swing, the validity of calling jazz an art form was questioned by nearly everyone (including important black intellectuals of the Harlem Renaissance such as Paul Robeson). As the relationship and trust among singers, bandleaders, and instrumentalists began to grow, however, the music evolved. In fact, it would not be long before swing—indeed, jazz itself—would be recognized by the international community as an authentic and exhilarating American art form.

Swing was the product of the growing collaboration among the members of the band, and in some ways reflected the greater social changes of the times. In swing, the tempo picked up, and greater emphasis was placed on personal expression during solos. In addition, many opportunities were opening up for historically disadvantaged segments of the population (women and African-Americans, for instance) to participate in the growing entertainment industry. This is not to say that there were equal rights guaranteed for all or that racism and sexism had evaporat-

ed from the national identity, but nonetheless the demographics of opportunity were beginning to shift.

The birth of swing can justifiably be placed in 1932, when Ivey Anderson recorded Duke Ellington's "It Don't Mean a Thing (If It Ain't Got That Swing)," predating swing as a national craze by nearly three years. The period between the recordings of this song and the last swing songs of 1944—the big band swing era—saw greater female participation in mainstream American music than ever before.

Some of the greatest female jazz singers of all time made their appearances in the first five years of the swing era. The immortal Ella Fitzgerald, who performed with Chick Webb's orchestra, took scat to new heights, while Billie Holiday played a major part in the evolution of the role of the female vocalist from band prop to legitimate solo artist.

Several of the swing era's prominent singers from 1935 on not only had in common the times and music but, strangely enough, the same first name. Helen Rowland, Helen Ward, Helen Humes, Helen O'Connell, and Helen Forrest were all important members of the second generation of female jazz singers.

Helen Rowland and Helen Ward share the honor of being the first of the Helens. Rowland toured with and sang on recordings of bandleaders

Opposite page: Ivey Anderson, flanked by Duke Ellington (to her right) and the rest of the band, was one of the greatest big band vocalists. Above: After the death of drummer-bandleader Chick Webb (at top), Ella Fitzgerald became the band's leader for over two years.

Fred Rich and Freddy Martin, while Ward was the first of several of Benny Goodman (1909–1986) headliners. Later she toured with Gene Krupa (1909–1973) and his band. Helen Ward's exuberant style inspired imitators like Martha Tilton and Edythe Wright, who both at different times replaced Ward in Benny Goodman's band.

Helen Humes, credited with being the most prolific of these five women, sang in six dis-

tinctly different musical styles, including jazz. Her study of the blues influenced her work in all other idioms.

The first of a long line of comedienne singers, the hilarious but often flat-pitched Helen O'Connell never gained acceptance as a jazz singer, but her place in jazz his-

From top to bottom: Helen Ward, Helen Humes, Helen O'Connell, and Maxine Sullivan.

tory is nonetheless important. She embodied the link between musical theatre (with its tradition of comedy) and jazz, and showed how the two forms could nourish each other. Musical comedy, which was always designed to entertain, and jazz, with its many technical demands, were brought together in ways that featured the strengths of both forms. (Another woman who also blurred the line between musical comedy and jazz was Maxine Sullivan [1911–]. She was the

Billie Holiday (1915–1959)

Billie Holiday was "discovered" in 1933 by producer John Hammond, who, upon hearing her once, summarily signed the Baltimore, Maryland, native to record with Benny Goodman's studio band. After this engagement she began a two-year tour with Teddy Wilson's combo.

In 1935, the jukebox came into existence and gave people in many parts of the country the opportunity to play the songs they liked whenever they wanted. Through this medium, the recordings of Billie Holiday quickly made her the most popular singer of the day.

After a long dispute with the ARC label over the distribution of the material she had begun writing, Holiday signed with the Commodore label in 1939. With the assistance of producers Benny Henighen and Milt Gabler, Holiday was finally able to express herself in her own words. The historic song "Strange Fruit," in which Billie laments the lynchings that continued to victimize African-Americans in the South, was the first to be recorded and distributed by her new label.

Holiday stayed with the small label until 1944, at which time the funds were running low at Commodore (producer Gabler was working a "day job" at Decca Records). Gabler tipped off Decca to the marketing potential of Billie Holiday's "Lover Man," which led to her signing with the larger label. She stayed with Decca for the next six years and recorded some of her finest material: "Crazy He Calls Me," "Porgy," and "My Man." She also had some of her own material recorded, including "God Bless the Child" and "Don't Explain."

During the last seven years of her life Holiday began working with producer Norman Granz (1918–), but due to her ever-declining health, her recordings from this period are inconsistent, ranging from brilliant to morbid. Drugs and drinking finally took their toll, ending the short, difficult life of the beautiful Billie in July 1959.

Helen Humes appeared with the Count Basie Orchestra at the Apollo Theatre in January 1939.

star of the 1939 Broadway smash *St. Louis Blues* and the headliner for John Kirby's and then Claude Thornhill's big bands.)

The last reigning Helen of swing was the sultry Forrest. Although she cut several sides with Artie Shaw, her work did not take on national prominence until World War II, when homesick GIs, in love with the lyrics of her songs and the sound of her voice, made Forrest one of the most successful big band singers near the end of the swing era.

Before, during, and after the period of the Helens, the great Ivey Anderson reigned. With Duke Ellington's orchestra, Ivey became one of the most important women of the era, singing some of Ellington's most memorable tunes, including "I Got It Bad (and That Ain't Good)" and "All God's Chillun Got Rhythm." All of her material sounds as vital today as it did when it was first recorded, which is ample testimony to her artistry.

Many other women made an impact on the era with varying degrees of professional and musical success. Bea Wain, for instance, was quite prolific. Her thick New York accent made songs like "A Gypsy from Poughkeepsie" (a hit she had with Gene Kardos' dance band) and "My Heart Belongs to Daddy" so unique that it has proved impossible for any other singer to cover the material. Wain also worked with Larry

Helen Forrest was, at different times, the lead singer for the orchestras of Benny Goodman and Harry James (pictured above).

Clinton and his orchestra in 1938, and in the following year began a long stint as the star of *Your Hit Parade*, a popular radio music revue.

Lena Horne (1917–), at the age of sixteen, made her first appearance in this era as a chorus girl at the Cotton Club in Harlem. She was soon thereafter taken under the wing of Noble Sissle, who at the time was leading his own orchestra. Charlie Barnet (1913–1991) also recognized the beautiful Horne's singing talent, and hired her to tour with

Helen Humes (1913–1981)

The recording career of Helen Humes began in 1927. Her voice then, as it would throughout her life, lent her an air of innocence that contrasted with her fiery character. The material that Humes chose to sing, much like the story she preferred to tell of her "boring" life, belied the naughtier side of her personality. Throughout her career, the self-described "sweet and lucky" Miss Humes was arrested for gambling (she lost several fortunes on the horses) and customarily polished off an entire bottle of whiskey before every recording date. Until her death, Humes admitted to none of her darker traits. "They'll never want to film the story of my life," she said. "I came from a happy family. . . . People don't like to hear about you when it's all happiness and contentment—you have to be drug [sic] through the mud and you have to be standing on the corner. But all I know is the good things in life."

More often than not her songs were about sex. On "Do What You Did Last Night," a song from her earliest recording session, Humes has the listener believing for nearly half of the cut that the song is about an angelic young woman, but by the beginning of the second verse her language becomes more suggestive, to say the least. By the end of the song, the singer has become downright lewd.

After the fourteen-year-old Humes completed her earliest session, her mother thought it best that Helen finish high school. After graduating, Humes joined tenor saxophonist Al Sears on a tour of Buffalo, Cincinnati, and New York. When the group disbanded, Humes and Sears joined Vernon Andrade's Renaissance Ballroom Orchestra.

Count Basie heard Humes sing with Sears and decided to sign her to front the Basie Orchestra. At Basie's request, Humes replaced Billie Holiday, and stayed with the band for four years. Her work with Basie includes recordings on the Okeh label, most of which are blues numbers fraught with the ever-present Humes double-entendre.

After leaving Basie's orchestra, Helen Humes recorded for Savoy, Decca, and Alladin. Her style of songs took a turn toward early rhythm and blues ("blues and jump" as it was then called), and in 1945 she recorded her greatest hit, the bouncy "E-Baba-Le-Ba."

At the end of the 1950s, Humes went back to her roots, singing jazz with Red Norvo's orchestra (on RCA) and then with composer-arranger Marty Paich. With interest in her career waning, she attempted her first comeback, traveling to Australia and France. Unfortunately, the tour was financially unsuccessful.

After the death of her mother in 1967, Humes grew tired of the music business and went to work in a munitions factory in Louisville, Kentucky. After six years of avoiding the music scene, she appeared at the Newport Jazz Festival. Interest in her work again mounted, leading to a gig at the famous New York club The Cookery in 1975. This date led to her recording *It's the Talk of the Town* on CBS Records. The headline of a *New York Times* review of the album read, "Helen Humes Discovered Again at 63."

As it turned out, Humes was at her most prolific when she was in her sixties, during which time she recorded for various English, French, and American labels. Humes died in 1981, five years after her successful comeback.

Lena Horne's most memorable song, "Stormy Weather," came from the movie of the same name. From right to left: Cab Calloway, Horne, and Bill Robinson performing in the movie.

his troupe for a brief period of time. She then earned a spot on the popular New York radio show *Chamber Music Society of Lower Basin Street.* In the following decade, Horne appeared in several movie musicals, such as *As Thousands Cheer, Stormy Weather,* and *Ziegfeld Follies.* Her work in musicals continued through the late 1950s, when she appeared in Arlen and Harburg's *Jamaica.* Her last stage appearance was in 1981, when she appeared in an autobiographical play set to music called *The Lady and Her Music.*

Teddy Grace, one of the greatest white, blues-oriented jazz singers of the swing era, left the scene as quickly as she had arrived on it. Jack Kapp produced several of her solo albums on Decca at the same time that Bob Crosby was making her the centerpiece of his band. She was also making headway into the motion picture industry at the time, appearing in her first feature film with Mel Hallett. Grace then joined

Ivey Anderson (1905–1949)

Born outside Oakland, California, on July 10, 1905, Ivey Anderson was the greatest singer of the greatest band in the history of jazz, the Duke Ellington Orchestra.

Anderson began her career in entertainment as a dancer in a show headlined by the legendary Mamie Smith that toured on the white vaudeville circuit. By the end of the 1920s, Ivey began touring as a singer, head-lining at both the New York and Los Angeles Cotton Clubs. She soon became the first black female singer to front an all-white big band, Anson Weeks and His Orchestra, which performed at the Mark Hopkins Hotel in San Francisco. Soon after, she moved to Chicago for a year-long engagement at the Grand Terrace with Earl Hines and His Orchestra.

Ellington caught Anderson's performance at the Terrace in February 1931 and immediately signed her out from under "Fatha" Hines. As the story goes, Ivey didn't think she was good enough to be with the near-legendary Duke, and only took the job after much reassurance from Ellington himself.

After eleven years and a Los Angeles appearance in Ellington's musical *Jump For Joy*, Anderson left the orchestra forever, unable to continue touring due to acute asthma. Her recording and performing careers became sporadic, and she appeared only occasionally in California and Mexico City.

Her attention turned to the running of a restaurant, the Chicken Shack, which she owned with her first husband, Marques Neal. She was later in the real estate business with her second husband, Walter Collins.

"They still talk about Ivey," Ellington said a decade after the end of Anderson's career with his band, "and every girl singer we've had since has had to try to prevail

Duke Ellington's favorite leading lady, Ivey Anderson, spent fourteen years with the band before retiring due to acute asthma.

over the Ivey Anderson image." Acute asthma took its final toll on December 28, 1949. Anderson died without leaving a will, leading to an extensive legal battle between her two former husbands.

an organization of volunteer performers (WACS), whose schedule was so rigorous that by the end of World War II she had lost her voice forever.

Two male artists of this era who were innovative and not merely Bing Crosby sound-alikes were Leo Watson (1898–1950) and Jimmy Rushing. The two served the cause of scat while fueling the future of jazz singers in general.

Strike

The death of the big band era had less to do with changing musical tastes than it did with the 1943 and 1948 union strikes. In an attempt to regulate the profits made by the recording companies, employees of the big bands began working together to fight the record industry. An inadequate percentage of the profits made it into the pockets of the musicians who had written and performed the music on the recordings. Although the workers' complaints—that their work was part of the profit-making process and should be proportionately rewarded—were legitimate, the end result was a decline

Vocal wizard Jimmy Rushing was the most popular male jazz singer in Britain and the United States from 1957 to 1959.

in the quality of the product and the demise of ensemble recordings (and eventually of the ensembles themselves).

The American Society of Composers, Authors and Publishers (ASCAP) and the American Federation of Musicians (AFM) began to wage its war against the recording industry. The union's greatest weapons,

Ella Fitzgerald had a smash hit in 1958 with her recording of "Satin Dolls," a classic jazz song penned by Billy Strayhorn and Duke Ellington.

bans and strikes, ultimately disenfranchised musicians and finally led to a growth of power in the recording industry. The labels went from creating a record of the times to making music history. By changing the focus from scouting for the greatest talent to finding the greatest market, the record industry sidestepped the union battle and won the popular music war. To this day, the music business in North America directly reflects the union's mishandling of the situation.

The union was dependent upon musicians refusing en masse to settle until their demands were met. The problem was that the AFM only represented certain kinds of musicians, namely instrumentalists working in established big bands, in clubs, and on Broadway. The result was that the majority of up-and-coming instrumentalists, not to mention vocalists, trying to break into the business were not at the negotiating table. ASCAP suffered from a twofold problem. Not only was its membership exclusive (like the AFM), but it had a main competitor vying for the right to make profits off the work of composers—Broadcast Music Incorporated (BMI). When ASCAP struck, the recording industry went to the competition.

ASCAP did make some gains in the struggle concerning royalties, and the AFM settled with each label separately during 1943 and 1944, but the damage had been done. Big band music would never thrive in the same way again.

In fact, music in general ultimately suffered from the emergence of the "artist and repertory" (A&R) representative. These free agents took the pressure off the labels as a whole by commandeering the change from artist-driven to market-driven music without involving the recording industry resources. Direct responsibility for the relationship between artists and the labels was now in the hands of a third party who had no wish to negotiate with the powerful, unionized bandleaders. Instead, the A&R representative carved out a market for vocal music, and began controlling singers and the material these singers covered.

Very few of the big band jazz singers were able to make the transition to the new market-driven music economy with their ego and craft intact. Each singer now dealt with the pressures that came with contract negotiations. Few dared to risk their place on a major label in the name of artistic integrity, and the result, in general, was the disappearance of great songs and great instrumental musicians from most recordings.

In the late 1940s and early 1950s, those singers who wished to continue contributing to the evolution of jazz—the music that had made them stars only a decade before—faced obscurity on minor labels and minimal financial success. Those who did succumb to the pressures of the A&R representatives, the singers for whom financial insecurity meant their families would suffer, were forced to sing inane tunes that made them a quick dollar but ultimately ruined their long-term credibility. The rise of the A&R representative proved a frightening point: if you make a package look pretty and tell everyone it's tasty, people will eat it up.

Francis Albert Sinatra began his solo career in 1943, and within a year became a film idol, recording star, and television actor.

The brightest male star to emerge from the strikes was Frank Sinatra (1915–   ). Fresh from the Tommy Dorsey band, Sinatra recorded "Sunday, Monday or Always," a tune that only recently had been covered by Bing Crosby for the latter's movie *Dixie*. The song that was supposed to be a "surefire hit" for Crosby was scooped out from under him during the ban by "Ol' Blue Eyes." Frank's discography, which stretches from that early period to a gold record in 1993, is a micro-history of jazz crooning in and of itself.

Victor, the label that carried both Dinah Shore (1917–1994) and Perry Como, was the last to settle with the AFM, finally coming to terms in 1944. Shore, who had gained some notoriety previous to the ban, was able to hit the charts in 1944 with "Tess's Torch Song." By 1951, she had begun making regular appearances on televison, as both a guest and host on talk shows. She was also an exuberant spokesperson for

Chevrolet and other companies. Her annually televised celebrity golf tournament and her weekday talk show, *The Dinah Shore Show*, stayed on the air from the mid-1950s until the mid-1980s.

Dinah Shore was one of the first female jazz solo singers to become a star following the devastating AFM and ASCAP strikes.

Singers of this period who were able to retain their musical integrity and still achieve some commercial success were few, but were for that reason important to the history of jazz singing. Two of these vocalists, Jo Stafford (1920–) and Margaret Whiting (1924–), exemplified the bare-bones practicality of post–World War II America with their straightforward, unadorned vocal styles. This no-frills approach was a welcome

respite from the frivolous vocalizing of many of the up-and-coming female singers of the time.

Doris Day (1924–), another talented vocalist of the era, was able to record in the jazz idiom in between her recordings of "high-pop" ditties. Some of Day's greatest work came from a session with a trio selected from the Harry James group. The album *Young Man with a Horn* (Columbia, 1950) shows off Day's tremendous virtuosity.

Doris Day's biggest hit, "Que Sera, Sera," later became the theme song to her popular television show.

At about the same time that the great Dinah Washington (1924–1963) was making the crossover from blues recordings to popular jazz ballads, Kay Starr made her entrance into jazz/pop recordings from an early career in country music. Although Starr achieved her greatest success during the 1940s, Washington would not make her popular splash until the mid-1950s.

Bebop

The widening rift between popular music and jazz that had first opened during the union strikes was liberating in many ways for those jazz instrumentalists who had seen their craft undermined by the industry's failure to grasp the incredible evolution that jazz had been

Dinah Washington, born Ruth Jones in Tuscaloosa, Alabama, began her singing career at the age of five after her family moved to Chicago, Illinois.

undergoing since its birth. The expectations of industry businessmen, finally divorced from the craft of jazz musicianship, sent American music in two entirely different directions.

Kay Starr (1922–   )

One of the greatest white, blues-based jazz singers of the post-ban era was Kay Starr. Born Katherine LaVerne Starks in Dougherty, Oklahoma, on July 21, 1922, Starr began her singing career at the age of nine by winning several amateur shows, all of which were broadcast in her hometown, Dallas, on WRR radio. After her family moved to Memphis, Starr earned her own regularly broadcast country music spot on WREC in 1934. She later moved her program to another local radio station, WMPS.

Bandleader Joe Venuti coincidentally heard Starr on WMPS while playing a Memphis gig. Venuti immediately asked her to tour with the band. Starr was again "discovered" in that same year by Bob Crosby, who also heard her singing on the radio, though this time it was with Venuti's orchestra. Crosby asked her to come to New York with his company. In June 1939, she began her very brief stint with Crosby on *The Camel Caravan* radio show.

At the request of her mother, Starr was soon back in Tennessee trying to finish high school. Within a month of her homecoming, however, Glenn Miller sent a telegram requesting that she stand in for the ailing singer Marion Hutton. In July 1939 Starr made her very first recordings, "Baby Me" and "Love With a Capital You," for the Bluebird label.

Following the Miller session, Starr made another attempt to finish high school. Again she was summoned, this time by bandleader Charlie Barnet, to tour and record. For the next three years, Starr worked with Barnet's band and, like many singers of the pre-micro-phone era, temporarily lost her voice trying to sing above the raging horn section.

Though her recovery from the rigors of touring was still incomplete, the young singer began working on a solo career, starting with an extensive tour of the United States and Europe. Several small labels recorded Starr during this period.

In 1947 Starr signed with Capitol Records and began working on an album with trumpeter-arranger Red Nichols (1905–1965). This collaboration brought her increasing success, and by August 1950 Starr was splitting the bill with the Nat King Cole Trio at New York's Paramount club. Capitol finally realized Starr's tremendous commercial potential and began putting together a large staff for her next and greatest album, *Bonaparte's Retreat*.

In 1955, Kay signed a contract with Victor Records that guaranteed her an astounding $250,000 against her royalties. Her first single from Victor, "The Rock and Roll Waltz," was so successful that the label began searching out a new type of singer—one who could balance the rhythmic elements of blues within a country music format. (This search, supposedly, eventually landed them none other than Elvis Presley.)

Starr returned to Victor in 1959 and, for the first time in a decade, recorded jazz material. As was to be expected of a jazz singer trying to achieve commercial success in the late 1950s, her records did not fare well, and Victor ultimately let her go. Undaunted, Kay Starr recorded through the late 1960s on minor labels like Gold Star, on which she was able to record jazz, the music to which she had contributed so much in her early career.

The musicians who continued to play and develop jazz began to espouse a freer, more individualistic approach to the music, an approach that eventually came to be called bebop. Still aware of the audience and the role of entertainment in music, many talented musicians embraced bebop because it engaged their intellect without compromising their sense of humor. A hybrid of Latin and African music, hinted at by the work of Charlie Parker (1920–1955) and brought to life by his friend and colleague Dizzy Gillespie (1917–1993), bebop was a welcome challenge to composers and musicians who had begun experimenting with rhythm, mode, and tone. In bebop, melody was no longer driven by the human voice, but by the piano, drums, and horns. The speed and technical complexity of the sounds that could be produced on these instruments began to define this new form of jazz.

The elimination of the voice as the centerpiece of a song led to an evolution in jazz singing. Bebop singing emphasized the instrumental (rather than the linguistic) qualities of the voice, which led singers to attempt incredible vocal feats and to approximate the sounds of other instruments through the use of nonsensical syllables. "Oop-Pop-A-Da" and "In the Land of Oo-Bla-De" are just two examples of such songs.

Out of Dizzy Gillespie's band came several of the successful scat singers who made the transition from swing to bebop. Joe Carroll and Kenny "Pancho" Hagood, two of the earliest singers to attempt vocals in the bebop style, and Ella Fitzgerald all credit the advances made by Leo Watson for their scat styles.

A sense of humor, among Leo Watson's greatest gifts, became the audience-legitimizing factor for bebop singing. The audiences who on first hearing scat had felt it was pure nonsense were astounded after a closer listen by the incorporation of outrageous progressions and rhythmic patterns into the jazz repertoire. Bebop singing was a phenomenon dizzying to singers as well as to the general audience; the inherent sense of levity took the edge off the insanity of bebop's superhuman vocalizing. Dave Lambert (1917–1966), Buddy Stewart (1921–1950), and Ella

Ella Fitzgerald (1918–)

The Virginia-born Ella Fitzgerald began her career as the first of many important winners of the Apollo Theatre talent contest in New York City. Thanks in part to an extensive knowledge of popular melodies and the know-how to incorporate those tunes into the structure of any song, Ella Fitzgerald was able to invent a singing style that contributed to the development of scat.

Ella Fitzgerald's earliest professional success, following her win at the Apollo, came at the age of seventeen with the recording of the hit "A Tisket A Tasket." At the time, she was the headliner for the renowned Chick Webb Orchestra. Then, at the ripe age of twenty-one, Fitzgerald became the band's leader when the legendary drummer-leader Webb (1909–1939) died of tuberculosis.

Fitzgerald was the leader of the outfit for two years before beginning her solo career. By 1945, Fitzgerald had established herself as the preeminent scat singer with her solo hit "Flying Home," which featured imita-

From left to right: Ella Fitzgerald, pianist Oscar Peterson, trumpeter Roy Eldridge, and drummer Max Roach rehearse for the evening's concert in Stockholm, Sweden.

tions of familiar jazz instrumental solos as part of her vocal riffs.

Ella Fitzgerald was also the only female vocalist to brave the strange new terrain of bebop singing. She began touring with Dizzy Gillespie's band in the mid- to late forties, expanding her vocal chops to include the new harmonies that were becoming the foundation of bebop. Fitzgerald married the leading bass player of the new form, Ray Brown (1926–), in 1947.

The 1950s brought Fitzgerald a recording contract with Decca and some of her most popular albums. In reaction to the lack of good new material that she was being presented with at the beginning of her career with Decca, she requested the opportunity to record the best songs of the best composers from Broadway. Decca bowed to her request for a short while, but her demands led to her departure from the company.

Between recording for Decca and Verve, Fitzgerald laid down dozens of show tunes. *Ella Sings Gershwin, The Cole Porter Songbook, The Rodgers and Hart Songbook, Irving Berlin, The Gershwin Songbook,* and *Hello Dolly!* are the classic collections of Fitzgerald's output. Nearly all of the cuts from these albums are the definitive jazz versions of Broadway's greatest hits.

Fitzgerald were witty as well as virtuosic leaders of the new school.

Buddy Stewart, a professional singer practically from birth, was the son of parents who had belonged to the vaudeville school of early twentieth-century performance. At first a banjo player, Stewart toured the vaudeville circuit, and by the age of fifteen was the vocalist with the roaming Jerry Livingston Dance Orchestra.

Dave Lambert, a tree surgeon and paratrooper turned professional drummer, worked with Johnny Long's Orchestra as an arranger directly following World War II. Not long after Lambert's arrival with the group, Long cast him as the band's rhythm singer and drummer. Both Lambert and Stewart, who began working together in Gene Krupa's band in 1945, survived the change from "sweet" to "hot" music, giving the pair a chance to show off their ground-breaking bop chops.

Vocalese

A logical progression from scat, vocalese involved the addition of lyrics and a story line to the instrumentally influenced (i.e., bebop) vocal solo. Although this concept had been tested early on in the history of jazz, the acceptance of "lyricizing" as a legitimate art form depended on the evolution of singers with the technical ability to accomplish the feat.

By 1939, Leo Watson was experimenting successfully with lyrics placed over existing sixteen-bar solo lines, but his early efforts had no immediate impact on vocalese as an institutionalized craft. In 1945, Dave Lambert and Buddy Stewart made an attempt at vocalese, and in the process made a name for themselves as a duet, but again the vocalese style was not validated either commercially or artistically. Not until 1950, when Sarah Vaughan and Eddie Jefferson recorded "Beautiful

Above: Sarah "Sassy" Vaughan recorded successfully until her death in 1990.
Opposite, top: A member of Dizzy Gillespie's band, Ella Fitzgerald was the only
female star of the bebop movement and was consequently at the forefront of the
evolution of vocal jazz. (That's Gillespie in the background.)

Sarah Vaughan (1924–1990)

Sarah Vaughan, the daughter of a carpenter and a laundress, began her involvement in music as a singer for the Mt. Zion Baptist Church in her hometown of Newark, New Jersey. Her technical training in music began at the age of six with studies on the piano and organ.

Like Ella Fitzgerald, Vaughan launched her professional career at the Apollo Theatre amateur contest. Singer Billy Eckstine caught her performance, and immediately recommended her to his bandleader, Earl Hines (1905–1989). Vaughan made her professional debut with Earl Hines' orchestra as a singer and second pianist in April 1943, again at the Apollo. Eckstine soon left Hines' band to form his own orchestra, and took Vaughan with him. Her first recording date was with Eckstine's group in a session that took place on December 31, 1944, on the Continental label.

In 1945, Vaughan left Eckstine and his orchestra to begin a solo career. At the urging of Dizzy Gillespie and Charlie Parker, she landed a contract with the Musicraft label, which in turn led to her first tour of the United States. At a gig at New York's Café Society club in 1946 she met her soon-to-be husband and manager, trumpeter George Treadwell. The two were married September 18, 1947. (Even after the couple's divorce, Treadwell continued to manage Vaughan's career for another two years.)

International recognition came in 1949, when Vaughan signed with Columbia Records. Columbia was able to secure plenty of airtime on the popular radio and television music programs of the day, as well as give her the opportunity to tour abroad.

Before and during her stint with Columbia, jazz fans had already begun hailing Vaughan as the most important singer of the era. *Downbeat* magazine's poll crowned her the greatest female singer in jazz from 1947 to 1952. Although her greatest success came in the late 1940s and early 1950s, Vaughan continued to sing beautifully until her death. Her last album, *Brazilian Romance,* a collaboration with Brazilian jazz master Milton Nascimiento, is a brilliant testament to the then seventy-six-year-old Vaughan's youthful spirit and mature musical vocabulary.

Sarah Vaughan sang with a fluidity and grace that brought beauty to even the most inane material.

Memories," did the concept of vocalese take hold with audiences and professional singers alike.

The traditionally lukewarm response audiences have had to vocalese stems from the fact that few singers were skilled enough to polish vocalese into an art. Thanks to Dave Lambert, the preeminent vocalese artist, "lyricizing" found popular acceptance and professional respect. Another person who rose to stardom because of Lambert's dedication to vocalese was the incredible Annie Ross.

Together with Dave Lambert and composer Jon Hendricks (1921–), Annie Ross was involved in vocalese's most important incarnation. The trio's album *Everybody's Boppin'* brought the concept of trio vocal jazz back into the limelight. Not since the Boswell Sisters and the Mills Brothers of the 1930s had the tight harmony and rhythmic complexity of multiple jazz voicings been as successful as it was as performed by Lambert, Hendricks, and Ross.

Annie Ross (1930–)

At the age of four, the singer and actress Annie Ross moved with her family to Hollywood, California, from her birthplace (Surrey, England) to begin a career in the motion picture industry. At the age of eight, she starred as a tiny Scottish character in *Our Gang Follies of 1938*. Ross followed up that cameo appearance with a role playing opposite Judy Garland in the movie *Presenting Lily Mars*. At the age of sixteen, Ross began studying acting in New York at the American Academy of Dramatic Arts.

At odds with her aunt Ella Logan (who raised her in the United States), Ross left for London, where she soon found work in the West End's theatre district. Within the following year she had decided to move to Paris, spending the majority of her time hanging out with the growing number of American jazz expatriates. Ross laid down her first recordings with a Parisian jazz group led by trumpeter James Moody (1925–).

While visiting New York the following year, she cut her first album for DeeGee Records (Dizzy Gillespie's short-lived label), accompanied by Blossom Dearie on piano, members of the Modern Jazz Quartet, and Kenny Clarke, her boyfriend at the time, on drums. Hits from that session, like "Moody's Mood for Love" and "Twisted," brought her to the attention of future collaborators Dave Lambert and Jon Hendricks.

Before real success could catch up to her, Ross had gone back to Europe to tour with Lionel Hampton's band. After a fight with Hampton in Sweden, Ross picked up and left for London, where she landed a starring role in the hit revue *Cranks*.

Because of Ross' theatrical success, Lambert and Hendricks finally made a real effort to work with her. After several failed recording sessions, with Ross as the choral coach of an all-female singing group, the three decided to try their voices as a jazz trio. The recordings that Lambert, Hendricks, and Ross made over the following few years placed them among the top three jazz vocal groups of all time.

The trio Lambert, Hendricks, and Ross was, as it turns out, originally a quartet with singer-actress Georgia Brown as the soprano. Brown, at the time of the foursome's existence, was Ross' roommate. Apparently Ross told Georgia Brown that everyone involved in the group wanted her out. Brown left town without ever saying goodbye. Only years later did Dave Lambert discover that Annie Ross had forced Brown out of the group behind their backs because she "wanted to be the only woman of the group."

Although Ross is best remembered for her work with the trio, her solo career has been substantial. Three albums, *Annie Ross Sings*, *Sing a Song with Mulligan*, and *A Gasser*, show off the vocal dexterity and clarity of pitch that have made her a historic figure in vocal jazz.

Lambert (right), Hendricks, and Ross are credited with both reviving and transforming the vocal jazz trio tradition.

The Vo-Cool Movement

In an era defined by the freneticism of "hot" jazz arose a school of musicians whose personalities dictated a different musical temperament—this new style of jazz was called, appropriately, Cool. The songs, from ballads to faster-paced swing numbers, covered by this new breed of musicians differed from the songs performed by the "hot" players only in interpretation. Taking the lead from earlier players like cornetist Bix Beiderbecke (1903–1931) and tenor saxophonist Lester Young (1909–1951), the musicians of the Cool school emphasized exploring the instrument's tone and its relationship to the player's personality rather than developing the ability to perform blistering licks.

The birth of Cool came in September 1948 at New York's Royal Roost club, when Miles Davis (1926–1991), former trumpet player for Charlie Parker, led a group in an evening of music that was more introspective than anything that had previously been explored by bebop or swing. From that evening was born a new era in jazz that was to redefine both instrumental and vocal interpretation.

It was not until the mid-1950s that singers, who had nearly been eliminated by the instrumental advances of bebop, found a home in Cool. What made the Cool singers different from their bebop counterparts was the matter of subtlety. Suggesting a vocal phrase, rather than the accomplishment of superhuman vocal feats, was the object of Cool singing. After an era of singers like Billy Eckstine and Sarah Vaughan, whose craft was based on the beauty of embellishment, the newest breed of singers began eliminating many vocal effects, specifically vibrato, the key element to most crooning. The emphasis of Cool singing was primarily on dynamics and clarity of pitch.

Trumpeter Chet Baker (1929–1988) inaugurated the Vo-Cool era with the release of the first of many albums on which he also sang. Although his technical approach was spare, his vocal tone was both suggestive and provocative. Throughout his life and career with Capitol Records, Baker was one of the more popular Cool performers.

Miles Dewey Davis, Jr., the son of a wealthy St. Louis dentist, attended the Juilliard School of Music.

The history of the successful Vo-Cool female singers began with the release of the 1954 hit song "Something Cool," by June Christy (1926–1990). Sales of the single were so good that Capitol decided to build an album around the song. By 1956, the album *Something Cool* had sold over ninety-three thousand copies. Christy's simple, melancholy vocal style imbued even the cheeriest of songs with incredible introspection.

Anita O'Day, a singer whose work was released only on minor labels until her entrance into Cool, surfaced as the leading female vocalist of the movement from 1954 forward. O'Day's rough-and-tumble lifestyle, as illustrated by her frank autobiography, *Hard Times, High Times*, made itself

Anita O'Day was notorious for her daring improvisational feats and racy social life.

apparent in her interpretations of jazz standards. O'Day's approach involved leaving the melody almost entirely, risking everything for the sake of interpretative freedom. Her consistently high-energy performances, along with her flights into melodic outer space, left audiences on the edges of their seats, curious as to whether she would make it through the material in one piece. The beauty of O'Day's style relied on the fact that she nearly always pulled off her wild musical interpretations.

Mel Torme, one of the all-time greats of male jazz singing, also had his greatest impact in this period. Torme, a native of Chicago, began his performance career as a child actor on radio spots and, a little later on, in the movies. His earliest singing job was with Chico Marx's all-juvenile dance band orchestra, a group put together by producers to pay off Marx's gambling debts.

Before Torme's enlistment in the army, he began work with a vocal group that he led called the Mel-Tones. The quartet recorded on both Jewell and Decca prior to his stint in the armed forces. After the end of World War II, he rejoined the group, and the trio signed with Musicraft, beginning their journey into modern jazz. In the years following the war, resentment within the music community over the unbelievable success of Torme's lesser works, along with the singer's own disgust with the popularity machine, caused Torme to focus on more substantial material and move away from recording-industry giants. For the sake of greater artistic control he began taking tremendous pay cuts to work on smaller, more artistically inclined labels.

The Vo-Cool movement has Torme's artistic integrity to thank for some of its greatest music. His work on the Bethlehem label is among the finest music of the decade. Albums like *Mel Torme and the Marty Paich Dek-Tette* and *Mel Torme Sings Fred Astaire* show off his ability to reconstruct compositionally any well-known tune and make it seem new again. On top of his remarkable vocal talents, Torme was an exceptional arranger and composer whose overall abilities would have been sacrificed on the bigger music labels.

The End of an Era

As A&R representatives continued to search for the largest possible markets throughout the 1950s, they soon discovered that the teenage consumer regularly bought (and still buys) more albums than any other identifiable group in North America. By focusing on teens' juvenile tastes and limited music education, the industry again redefined popular music in order to turn a healthy profit. The relationship between popular music and jazz, which had been awkward for over a decade, was finally and completely finished.

Three elements that the music of the younger generation continued to share with the music of their parents were the singer as the front person of the band, the basic AABA song structure, and a proliferation of dance

Anita O'Day (1919–)

Anita O'Day began her career as a singer in her hometown of Chicago, Illinois, at the now famous Three Deuces club in 1939 with Max Miller's band. She joined Gene Krupa's outfit in the early part of 1941, and toured and recorded with the band extensively for the next two years. It was with Krupa that O'Day began amassing an early following of avid fans. Her first hits, "Let Me Off Uptown" and "That's What You Think," came during those years with Krupa. From 1944 to 1945, she worked with Stan Kenton (1911–1979), recording another of her hits, "And Her Tears Flowed Like Wine."

After another short stint with Krupa, O'Day began a solo career. She toured and recorded extensively throughout the 1950s, but did not have another day in the international limelight until her tremendous performance at the Newport Jazz Festival in 1958. In 1959 she toured Europe with Benny Goodman's orchestra, and landed a starring role in her only film, *The Gene Krupa Story—Jazz on a Summer's Day.*

Although Anita O'Day's career began during the last few years of the swing era, her greatest influence came as a leader of the Vo-Cool movement. A penchant for risk, both melodically and personally, became her trademark. A long-standing addiction to heroin led to heart problems by the late 1960s, but fortunately for herself and the history of jazz, O'Day was able to beat the addiction before it could take its ultimate toll. Anita continued to record sporadically through the 1980s.

rhythms. A fourth and key ingredient of the new pop, which legitimized the music in the ears of consumers, was the blues scale. This new sound, of course, was rock and roll.

The reign of Frank Sinatra as the greatest male singer in North America was succeeded by that of Elvis Presley, whose Delta blues–derived sound and brash, youthful style spoke to the newly discovered market. The two singers shared the same vocal traits: those of the blues-based crooning balladeer. Similarly, a brash Southern singer named Brenda Lee (1944–) assumed the torch of female popular singing from the likes of Doris Day and Dinah Shore. Although Lee also sang popular ballads, the vocal similarities between Lee and the women who had been instrumental early in the history of popular music are fewer than those between Sinatra and Presley. The jazz-influenced repertoire of the 1940s had been supplanted by rhythm and blues and rock and roll as the popular music of North America.

The important technical elements lost in the transition were the craft of orchestral arrangement, intricate vocal technique, and the instrumental vocabulary that had been built upon by one musician after another during the first fifty years of the twentieth century. The musicians who continued to hone their craft in "pure" jazz from the 1940s forward began facing their own internal battle concerning the evolution of their music. The rift caused by this heated debate split the music into separate camps once again, ultimately leading to the disintegration of the music's core audience.

Instrumental musicians still interested in the evolution of the music focused on the expansion of song form and scale. Miles Davis continued to explore these new realms with ground-breaking albums like *Kind of Blue*, which introduced listeners to preeminent players like John Coltrane (1926–1967), Cannonball Adderly (1928–1975), Bill Evans (1929–1980), Paul Chambers (1935–1969), and James Cobb (1929–).

The elimination of the human voice was, in this school of jazz, complete. The vocabulary of instrumental music continued to expand throughout the 1950s, moving further away from the preconceived notions of melody. Continuing musical innovation drove the music toward the avant-garde. Along with Coltrane, several "out" players ("out" is used in jazz to imply the move away from conventional form) emerged, changing the relationship between the performers and audience forever. Archie Shepp (1937–), Ornette Coleman (1930–), and, later on, Cecil Taylor (1930–) and Bill Dixon (1925–) created a music that had nothing to do with the concept of entertainment for its own sake.

The Vo-Cool movement, begun in the mid-1950s, extended only into the early 1960s. The singers who came up during and after the reign of Cool primarily remained true to the music of the "good old days." The songs that began to be forced into the category of "standard" were not a part of jazz at all, and had to be revised to fit the idiom. No matter how much jazz singers tried to update and repopularize the idiom they so loved, the "jazzing up" of songs from the 1950s and 1960s only made more apparent the decline of the jazz vocalist.

Unable financially to support a band behind them, many singers accompanied themselves on the piano. Rose Murphy (1913–1989), Nellie Lutcher (1915–), Nina Simone (1933–), Blossom Dearie (1928–), Dorothy Donegan (1924–), Mary McPartland (1920–), and Shirley Horn belonged to an era defined by necessity. If female singers were to continue practicing their art they had to be, for the most part, self-sufficient.

The British Invasion of the late 1950s may have been as sweeping as it was because of the fact that American listeners in general were tired of contemporary popular music. Jazz took a staggering blow, falling a distant third in popularity behind the British and American rhythm and blues performers. From this time forward, the number of female singers interested in pursuing a jazz career, which offered no guarantees, slimmed to almost nil. Those few who did suffer the terrain made a lasting, and possibly final, mark on the history of female jazz singing.

One woman whose rise in popularity came in the midst of the popular drought was Abbey Lincoln. Over a period of thirty years, Lincoln reinvented herself several times. Her rise to respectability and autono-

Abbey Lincoln (1930–)

Abbey Lincoln, born Anna Marie Wooldridge in Chicago, Illinois, is considered by many to be the greatest ballad singer of the late 1950s. Her stunning beauty, along with her unique vocal style, had caught the attention of Liberty Records during the mid-1940s, beginning her career as a pop singer (at the time, Lincoln went by the name Gaby Lee). The movie industry saw some potential in her for the silver screen and hired her to star in Frank Tashlin's movie *The Girl Can't Help It*.

Lincoln began recording with Riverside Records in 1957, and produced three of the most retrospective albums of the day. The album *That's Him*, specifically, hearkened back to jazz music of the 1920s. Stardom and alcohol took their toll very quickly. Sobriety and a fourth career phase came with an introduction to her soon-to-be husband, drummer and composer Max Roach (1925–). She changed her name again, this time to Aminata Moseka, and cleaned up her habits. The two musicians' respect for one another soon led to their historic collaboration on politically oriented material such as *Freedom*.

Lincoln's unconventional choices concerning pitch and tone, along with her polyrhythmic approach to singing lyrics, make her recordings from all her incarnations as dramatic and innovative today as the day she recorded them.

Carmen McRae, in the shadow of Sarah Vaughan and Billie Holiday at the beginning of her professional life, did not gain the popularity she so deserved as a pianist and singer until later in her career.

my came with the album *That's Him* (1957), in which she chose to ignore completely the concept of musical evolution and return to the sounds of the 1920s and 1930s, breathing new life into the earliest work of African-American stars like Ethel Waters and Florence Mills.

Another performer who began her career in the latter days of swing and continued to be popular even into the early 1960s was pianist-singer Carmen McRae (1922–). She had her greatest success in the late 1950s, while recording with Decca, with the timeless albums *By Special Request* (1955) and *When You're Away* (1959).

The 1960s saw the rise of two female performers, Peggy Lee (1920–) and Betty Carter. While both remained faithful to the Tin Pan Alley song

Betty Carter (1929–)

The last of the essential female jazz singers arrived on the scene just when jazz singing was declared officially dead. A native of Detroit, Betty Carter was born Lillie Mae Jones in 1929. Although she grew up singing, playing the piano, and arranging choral music for church, she did not begin a recording career until the age of twenty-six. Her earliest work in the field of music included talent shows, bar gigs, and, in 1947, a big first opportunity with the Charlie Parker Quintet.

On a dare from a friend, young Betty Carter introduced herself to Lionel Hampton in the early 1950s and, upon being hired, left home for the first time. Over the next two years, she toured with his orchestra, but, like every other singer who came through Hampton's camp, she was fired on several occasions. At the request of Lionel's wife, Carter was rehired almost as often as she was given the boot.

Over the next twenty years, Carter turned up on recordings as a stand-in pianist and singer. Her work through the 1950s included recordings for King Pleasure and Ray Bryant, and a concert date as pianist with the Miles Davis Quintet at the Apollo. Carter recorded rhythm and blues for the first time with the Texas label Peacock, and then with Ray Charles (1930–). That collaboration led to the duet album *Ray Charles and Betty Carter*.

The rock craze of the 1960s finally forced Betty Carter out of pop-music mayhem entirely. Her next album, *Inside Betty Carter*—a foray into modern jazz—marked a major turning point in her career. By the late 1960s, she had begun her own recording label, Bet-Car.

Bankable professional recognition came not with Carter's work as a jazz singer, but as an actress, when she appeared in the Brooklyn show *Don't Call Me, Man*. Since then she has used what power she has acquired to promote the finest young instrumental talent in jazz. In addition, Carter herself continues to perform to this day.

Peggy Lee, pictured here with Louis Armstrong, received an Academy Award nomination for her tremendous acting and singing in the 1956 film Pete Kelly's Blues.

standards, their styles were quite different. Lee tried on many occasions to update the jazz sound to fit the marketing ploys of the current music scene, while Carter remained true to the history of innovation in jazz, interpreting songs in a near-avant-garde vocal style.

From the 1960s to today there has been no apparent heir to the long tradition of jazz vocalists. Those with the vocal dexterity to cover previously established styles of jazz have always done so, singing standards as an homage to the music that, if the music industry had not changed so dramatically over the previous decades, would perhaps have been

Although she is revered as a jazz singer, Betty Carter achieved her earliest popularity as a vocal artist by recording an album of popular duets with Ray Charles.

Besides being a gifted musician, Betty Carter is also a skilled businesswoman who owns and runs the record label she founded, BetCar.

their home. But the spirit of innovation—which has always characterized jazz in its many manifestations—has not been part of the jazz vocal tradition for decades. In addition, the imminent death of the Broadway musical, the long-standing link between female vocalists and the jazz idiom, and the gradual overall extinction of jazz as an evolutionary art form may eventually leave the female jazz singers without an audience or a contemporary selection of songs.

The decades-long vacuum in vocal jazz has served at least to canonize the achievements of the remarkable women who changed the face of the entertainment map through their dedication and talent. The music of these singers, from Ethel Waters to Betty Carter, is an aural history of the twentieth-century musical experience.

Suggested Listening

Bailey, Mildred. *Harlem Lullaby* (British Living Era)

The Boswell Sisters. *The Boswell Sisters* (Patricia Records, Denmark)

Carter, Betty. *'Round Midnight* (Atco, Japanese Atlantic)

Day, Doris. *Doris Day and Les Brown: Best of the Big Bands* (Columbia)

Fitzgerald, Ella. *Duke Ellington* (Verve)

Holiday, Billie. *Billie Holiday*, Volumes 1-9 (ARC)

Humes, Helen. *Count Basie, 1938–1939* (Classics)

Lincoln, Abbey. *That's Him* (Riverside [Fantasy])

McRae, Carmen. *Take Five with Dave Brubeck* (Columbia Special Products)

O'Day, Anita. *Pick Yourself Up* (Verve)

Ross, Annie, Dave Lambert, and Jon Hendricks. *Everybody's Boppin'* (Columbia)

Shore, Dinah. *The Best of Dinah Shore* (Curb)

Stafford, Jo. *Collector's Series* (Capitol)

Starr, Kay. *Kay Starr, Collector's Series* (Capitol)

Washington, Dinah. *Dinah Washington: 1943–1945* (Danish Official)

Waters, Ethel. *On Stage and Screen* (Columbia Special Products)

Wiley, Lee. *I've Got You Under My Skin: The Complete Young Lee Wiley, 1931–1937* (Vintage Jazz Classics)

Suggested Reading

Collier, James Lincoln. *Jazz: The American Theme Song*. New York: Oxford University Press, 1992.

Crow, Bill. *From Birdland to Broadway*. New York: Oxford University Press, 1992.

Feather, Leonard. *The Encyclopedia of Jazz*. New York: DaCapo Press, 1960.

Friedwald, Will. *Jazz Singing*. New York: Collier Books, Macmillan Publishing Company, 1992.

Woll, Allen. *Black Musical Theatre: From Coontown to Dreamgirls*. Baton Rouge: Da Capo Press, 1989.

Photography Credits

Index